Bleed, My Heart

Kilayla Pilon

BookLeaf Publishing

Presentation by *BookLeaf Publishing*

Web: www.bookleafpub.com

E-mail: info@bookleafpub.com

ISBN: 978-93-95784-07-8

First edition 2022

ACKNOWLEDGEMENT

To my Nanny, my best friend
To my Mum, who saved me again

Shadows Above

In this water, a gentle blue
A soft wind blowing, the calm passing through
See not the cascading shadow above
While seeking new and effervescent love
Watch how to make your blood will flow
Your veins, spewing free
Know that the love is through
The bitter stab of cruelty, true

Blood

Shattered wounds and scattered scars
A scrapped metal collection of contraband
Bloodied tissue, blood shot eyes
All I say and all I ask
Please do not advice
I have no fight left

Muse, my blade

I hear the beckoning sirens call
Coming from the silver blade
It was my muse,
My scarlet downfall
And while the scars of come to fade
The memories will forever remain
The days the blade kissed my skin
And fed the monster deep within

Sightless

Left out of sight
You lurk in the corners of my panicked, frantic
mind
Waiting, haunting, ready for a cruel embrace
And I am lost to this cruel rage
An enemy, a victim
While also partially a dinner
Perhaps I am nothing more
Than a passing, weak whisper

Sinking

I dream of falling autumn leaves
The canopy of these beautiful trees
A hidden goal so far away
The leaves, they start to decay
And I hope so to be away
Finding myself sinking as the branches sway
I dream of collapsing into the gray
Oh, I've made it another day

Lost Embrace

Never held in an embrace
The tender love, such a strange sensation
The love, how it sent fear shooting through me
Like the vibrant flash a lightning strike
Yet in your arms I found anew
A gentle, soft part of my heart
Belonging to you, no worlds apart

Catastrophic

Tired and alone
My mind so focused, turned to stone
I cannot think a sense of freedom
Trapped in a mind, perhaps participants
Of catastrophic treason
Against the love I can no longer feel
Tired and alone,
There is no longer a place called home

Desperate, gentle motion

Hungered through violent desire
I swallow your word that bring me down under
Like the waters of an ocean divine
So desperate for love of gentle motion
I never noticed the knife
And the bloodied spill into the ocean,
Falling

Exhausted Eyes

Tired eyes with exhausted circles,
A broken grin, a weak smile
I knew one day it would come
I, the wearied pilot, the crew of lonely few
It was that I knew would come
To wash upon the cragged bay, the rocks against
the hull
Just as your touch tore my heart
The crash of the boat led me
To be melt into the sea, less failure be the only
way

Crimson Smears

Smears of crimson on my wrist,
Painting in smears as the drops fall to the floor
The desperate, yearning for love
So I found it here,
In the silver sliver pain and yet wondered why
How had I ended up with such a yearning to die?

Artistic sorrow

Lines of artistic sorrow, the water low within the
porcelain home
Dripping to the linoleum floor,
Oh, this is nothing new
For with a silver precious tool, the blood
released anew,
Perhaps one day I'll be one of the lucky few
For my words they come forth
A bubbling brook of sorrows station
Remember the artistic design, I have fallen into
the pit of annihilation

Gentle river

Rivers run on sorrowed tears
Forgotten following of the fears
Traveling past the bubbling bank
Unforgotten, my heart sank
Like a sorted river run.
Or a fool in the glum
This darkness that besets the rolling
Gently passing waves whilst falling
My tears have kept the river near
For I live here, buried in fear

Closed eyes

If I were to lie my head
Close my eyes to this sense of dread
Perhaps this night would be my last
I found myself hoping fast
For mortality, it is a word
That shakes the mightiest of the herd
Yet for someone such as me
It breaks me free from malady

Drastic, sorrow

Exhausted eyes, forlorn emotion
Drastic waves, a fluid motion
Singled hearts that cave with death
Alone in hummingbird fluttering heartbeat
I sit and wait, restless
For whence the emotion shall flood, endless

Poetic canvas

I remember you like shades
Of pastel blue and violet hues
The work of art from a canvas and brush
Your eyes so gentle and your skin
Filling me with sin, yes
I remember the shades
Of you

Monstrous

I cannot hear nor can I see
These monstrous words that torment me
In the shadows lay in wait
Vicious tones and berserk fate
Ears open to the sound
Yet wishing I could not be found
They lurk with mismatched toothy grin
Perhaps a sign I am a child of sin
One day their breath will fall on my flesh
Devour my once gentle soul, fresh
Their hunger and wait finally saited
While torn apart, I am obliviated

Overcast Heart

17

Desperation at the helm of my overcast heart
Patterns scrawled in red upon every part
My legs a war zone
My wrists a battle wearied home
I'll never forget the metals kiss
It makes me feel so less alone

Pink Scars

To those battle wearied, the brave
Skin decorated with pink welt scars
Though some are faded, a pale tone
These scars earned by gasping for breath,
yearning for home
The smears of blood, choking each breath
Stained skin, forgotten not
We say goodnight,
Your sacrificed not for naught

Sunset shadows kiss my skin
These bruised eyes holding stagnant within
Exhaustion sitting heavy as I lie in wait
I am so forlorn of this fate
For stories seek a different ending
Flowing laughter, joyous mocking with so few
defending
I can hear the sirens call
Your fear consumes me, I cannot fall

I do not know this beginning rule
Where a breath starts a story,
Yet I do not know what the middle holds
Shivering hands that scribble notes
Panicked breaths catching in my throat
This middle I do not know,
The end is the only place to go
Chaos caused by my trembling hands
I do not know this beginning rule
And I don't believe I'm ready for the throw

A gasping breath that comes from me
Deep, profound, hiding profanity
I walk the streets of blue and green
The ocean open, where I am free
For to the gasping laughter fed to me
The idea of love, the idea of we
And while we dance beneath the moon
I understand, perhaps
I am one of the forgotten few